"Everything you love is very likely to be lost, but in the end, love will return in a different way."

— **Franz Kafka**

A Bagel and a

Boiled Egg

*

J.S. Davis

For Mum and Dad – and all they left behind…

INTRODUCTION

When I sat down to write this book, my goal wasn't simply to tell a Covid-based story of coming to terms with and acceptance of grief. Nor was it just a cathartic attempt at getting it all out. I just wanted to write it all down and see if it took some shape, and if other people could associate with the mess of having loved ones die at a time when we couldn't stand 200 centimetres from each other, without some jobsworth with a tape measure and hi-vis jacket ushering us along.

I tried other titles, to see if they fit: *Death in the Time of Covid*, *How to Die at a Social Distance*, etc. In the end, I settled on something a little more abstract and which amused me. All of these rituals that dying as a Jew throws at you felt very amusing, at a time when all I wanted to do was cry. Eating a bagel and a boiled egg frantically purchased from a Tesco Express, immediately before my mum's funeral, was one of those "you-couldn't-make-it-up" rituals. The post-mortem ritual dance that, not just the religious but, we all face (often blindly), was genuinely amusing at times, albeit darkly so.

This story is for everyone who didn't have a clue what to do, didn't know how to cope, or simply did nothing to avoid it all. For and about those who maybe need to find something funny in the unbearably painful time they've faced.

Find the funny moments and keep hold of them – they'll get you through.

Chapter 1

Day One: The Call

"I will be in trouble for leaving here. Please don't ask questions." She palmed the meds from her mouth and threw them onto the floor. "Shhhh, don't say anything in front of them; they're listening to everything."

The nurses busied themselves with other more docile residents, spooning food into their mouths, as their empty eyes rolled about their heads. My mum's eyes darted from side to side in a kind of panic, looking for an escape from the torment inside, convinced that there was some kind of plot to keep her in the nursing home against her will, and that the drugs were their not-so-subtle means of resident control.

She shuffled back toward her room. At this stage, the cancer had caused such a growth in her abdomen that she had a beach ball-sized distension soldered to her frail frame. A snowman-cum-scarecrow physique is probably the best way to describe the combination of tumours, cysts, ascites and an inability/unwillingness to eat.

She held my hand and asked me not to leave.

The only resident with some semblance of capacity walked over to us. "I'll look after her. Don't worry."

"I'll see you soon, Mum, but I have to leave now."

"Please don't leave."

"I'm sorry, Mum, I have to go." I didn't have to go; I wanted to. I couldn't be there any longer.

Those were the last words I said to her. The next time I saw her she was dead.

After four hours or so in the summer heat, when we arrived she was visibly rotting.

The call came around midday. The name of the nursing home flashed up on the caller I.D. and I picked up. It was one of the nurses.

"I don't know how to say this – your mum has died."

I almost appreciated the bluntness. I hate the term "passed away"; it means nothing – not literally or figuratively. It's barely English.

You can never really prepare yourself for that call; even if it's wholly expected, it still comes as a complete shock. I don't know what my initial response was; I still don't remember what I said. Did I mishear them? Was it real?

I called back and asked some questions that I clearly wasn't able to ask at the first attempt. She WAS dead.

Numbness ensued and I tried to shake off the stress-blank, which felt like someone had thumped me in the head, rendering me unable to think, speak or remember.

My wife, Rezanne, stared knowingly through me. Her fingers curled into her palm, resting on her chin as she held back the tears.

I ran through lists in my head: what to do next? My thoughts were jumbled, and they raced back and forth in panicked incoherence. I phoned the funeral director and asked what to do. I had no idea.

Given my mum's miraculous cancer survival (told she had 3-6 months to live in March 2018; survived until July 2020), I had been granted plenty of time to contact funeral directors and make arrangements. I had played through dress rehearsals of this moment in my head: what would I do; who would I call; how would I react? Despite the fact that I thought I was prepared for her death, the reality of it was that all I had prepared was a number for the funeral directors, saved on my phone.

We packed and made our way to the nursing home. We drove in silence; I couldn't speak. I just didn't know how to communicate. The sense of knowing and expectancy, rather than preparing me for this moment, had created an incredible sense of looming. This looming, anxious cloud now poured down on me. It smothered me, rendering me incapable of speech or coherence. I was drowning in thought. Tears filled my eyes as I turned off at junction 13 on the M4. Not long to go now.

I pulled up at the nursing home gates, and my brother pulled in no more than a few minutes later, with my dad strapped into the front seat. The funeral director's van was parked up to one side.

Travis came on the radio – a blast from the past, maybe twenty years ago; the first album my brother ever bought. Come to think of it, my mum probably bought it for him. "Driftwood" fittingly played on. I turned it up for my brother to hear, and we smiled at one another before heading to reception. My dad ambled his way out of the car, grappling onto anything that looked like it might hold his weight, regardless of whether it would. His increasing immobility had led to a considerable amount of weight gain, mainly around the belly and cheeks. His legs remained spindly, due to the lack of exercise and general use.

We P.P.E.-ed, and Rezanne and I decided to head up first. My brother would then wait with my dad, so that we could assess whether or not my dad could cope with what we were about to see. We were ushered through to her bedroom, receiving sharp glances from scrub-clad staff as we passed through the hallways

– followed by sharp, downward-averted stares as they realized where we were headed. All heads seemed to at once bow in succession as we neared her room, then face away to avoid the awkwardness.

She lay rigid, feet bolt upright, head more or less the same, as rigor mortis slowly set in. Her eyes stared upward, searching, one slightly more than the other, like a broken doll. Her mouth bubbled and her nightgown was covered in a coarse, brown spew.

I stared at her lifeless, grey body, unsure of what to do next. Rezanne and I edged closer and bent over her. The brown bubbles surfaced, one by one in her mouth, and popped, releasing a bile-like substance down her chin. I found some tissue and wiped her mouth.

Her one eye squinted at me, as if she were trying to see me one last time. The other stared in the other direction, avoiding eye contact with me altogether.

"Do I close her eyes? What do I do?" I whispered across to Rezanne.

"I don't know," she replied. "I'm not sure what you're supposed to do."

I decided to wait for Nate to arrive before doing anything. I hurried downstairs, toward reception, and told him to make his way up, but that Dad couldn't come; it would be too much for him to take.

"Dad, you can't; you don't want to see her like this. It's okay to remember her how she was. I know you want to see her, but you have to trust me. You won't be able to cope if you do. Okay?"

"But… I want to see her one last time. Can I at least take a photo of her?"

"No, Dad, it's not right."

"Look, I'll agree to come up if you let me take a photo."

"Dad, I'm sorry, you can't."

I'm not sure what made him want a photo of my dead mum to remember her by, and I'm not going to attempt to sift through the vague logic in his thought process at such a griefstricken point in his life, but it was, suffice to say, an odd request. Eventually, he relented, and I led my brother upstairs, back through the winding linoleum corridors. Bumping into the manager on the way up, we asked him to look after Dad whilst we made our way back up to the room.

Wails echoed out from the room next to my mum's, as her neighbour struggled with crippling dementia, in what appeared to be a vain attempt to scream herself out of her own anguish. Completely divorced from reality, we saw her rolling from side to side in her bed, making more of a squawking sound than a scream or a wail.

We opened the partly-closed door and made our way in. Rezanne sat hunched over my mum's bedside, tears rolling down what could be seen of her face between mask and cheek. Nate pinched the bridge of his nose and tried to catch his breath. I put my arm over his shoulder and then Rezanne did the same. We cried – we all cried. My mum watched on, eyes still open, as her children grieved, participating by proxy in this strange ritual. It felt as if she were a live participant in this process, until the funeral director would remove her body to be prepared for burial.

"I need to close her eyes."

No one responded, just consented by omission to what needed to be done.

I moved my gloved hands toward her face and, with thumb and middle finger, closed both eyes at once. "Bye, Mum," I mumbled.

They popped back open. One by one, each eye went back to the same position it had taken, the right eye half-closed in a squint, the left fully open, staring upright and slightly to her left.

"They won't close," I muttered, through tears.

I tried again and again, but the same thing happened: her mouth bubbled and her eyes refused to shut. One last act of indignation: a refusal to appear dead, despite her morbid state. In silence, I stopped. Instead, I pulled the sheet up over her face, to hide us from her stares. The sheet was level with her forehead when it caught on her turgid feet. I grabbed at the base of the sheet and yanked it free.

Her jewellery. The funeral director had told us that we needed to take off all of her jewellery before she was taken to burial preparations. Jewish tradition does not allow for anything other than a shroud to be buried with the dead, I was told.

"I can't do it."

So, Rezanne volunteered.

I pulled the sheet back and Rezanne delicately removed her earrings – a gift from her mother, that I do not believe she had ever removed, in forty or so years.

"Is she wearing a watch? Shit, she's wearing a watch, isn't she? It will be on her right hand."

We lifted the side of the sheet closest to us and saw that her arms had begun to blacken. She was so emaciated that there was simply bone and skin, no flesh. Just blackened skin hanging off lifeless bones. Rezanne lifted her arm, ever so slightly, to create an angle to remove the watch. She unclipped the thin, gold-coloured Sekonda and slid it slowly off her right arm. Placing her arm back against her side, we pulled the sheet back over her body and gently placed it atop her head.

We sat for a while, quietly contemplating the nature of what had just happened. Then, I slowly gathered her belongings, scattered haphazardly around the room, and ushered Rezanne and Nate out. I looked back at her sheet-shrouded body and muttered one last goodbye.

*

My father died from Covid-19 some six months later, in early January. He was very old, and already had nearly everything wrong with him that could be, before the diagnosis, so he didn't really stand a chance.

3) I will request an up to date echocardiogram to assess your cardiac function due to exertional breathlessness

4) If you have further falls, I would recommend your GP start bone protection to prevent possible fracture

Past Medical History

1) Admission October 2017 with left parafalcine acute subdural haematoma following a fall

2) Atrial fibrillation
   a. Warfarin stopped in October due to above. Advised to hold for 6 weeks then consider restarting

3) Ischaemic heart disease
   a. Inferior STEMI 2006: PCI with DES to RCA
   b. CABG + mitral valve repair 2013

4) Hypercholesterolaemia

5) Pacemaker (DDD) for syncope 2010

6) Mild left ventricular systolic impairment and left ventricular hypertrophy (echo 2013)

7) Prostate cancer
   a. On LHRH agonist
   b. For PSA monitoring every 6-12 months
   c. Bone scan negative 2014

8) Colonic polyp 2012

9) Sigmoid diverticular disease

10) Stroke 2013

11) Bipolar disorder (mainly depression)

12) Gout

13) Hypothyroidism

Current Medications
1) Aspirin 75mg OD
2) Bisoprolol 2.5mg OD
3) Levothyroxine 50mcg OD
4) Priadel MR (lithium) 400mg ON
5) Venlafaxine 150mg BD
6) Pravastatin 20mg ON
7) Tamsulosin 400/Dutasteride 500 OD
8) Allopurinol 100mg OD
9) Mirabegron MR 25mg OD
10) Zolpidem 2.5mg ON
11) Senna as and when

This letter has been generated from SystmOne

The list of ailments and prescribed medication, provided by the G.P., was as shown above. Heart disease, cancer, bipolar, a stroke and gout, to top it off! Almost impressive that he remained semi-functional!

Our cat had died a couple of weeks earlier, and we buried my father with the same shovel we used to bury Poppy – and the same shovel we used to bury our first cat, Pushkin. I'm not really sure how our cats' names jumped from Russian-Jewish poet to popular millennial girl's name/November lapel accessory. No member of the deceased household could avoid the dubious privilege of being buried with the Davis family spade.

Due to Covid-related restrictions, the cemetery operated a bring-your-own-shovel policy during my mother's burial; however, a shovel-sharing policy was deemed acceptable for my father, by the powers that be in the cemetery world. Of course, given the Judaic tradition of taking turns to shovel dirt onto the coffin of the semi-buried, this led to some difficulties, as some more than others were willing to shovel-share (whether that be the cemetery's shovel or our own). The solution being that a series of elderly Jews queued up to lob fistfuls of dirt at my mother, carefully socially distancing themselves from one another throughout the dirt-throwing ritual. Some braver members of the tribe flouted guidance and self-regard, and braved infection, after I poured an entire bottle of sanitizing gel over the shovel's handle and shaft. The handle, now covered in a sticky mess of dirt and gel, was clearly much dirtier than before.

The rabbi kept his distance in black, plastic-gloved hands, black mask and a black, wide-brimmed hat. I have still never seen the face of the rabbi who presided over the burial of my mother and father, as the faceless Scot led the prayers.

My father's funeral took place at a point in time when two thousand people per day were dying of Covid across the U.K., which led to a number of ceremonial difficulties – the main difficulty being the attendance of a rabbi.

Before agreeing to attend, peak-pandemic, the McRabbi gave me a caveat: I could "nort mainshen Co-vid – nort in erny sayrcumstarnces." His wife wouldn't allow him to attend if she knew my father had died from Covid – and she may turn up, to make sure all was in order.

I agreed, then chose to wholly ignore his request. Should all attendees be given alternative causes of death, because the rabbi was scared of his wife? She sat in the car throughout the service, blissfully unaware, likely thinking that my elderly father had died peacefully in his sleep.

Don't underestimate the Jewish male's capacity for cowardice and ridiculousness in the face of the Jewish female; a policy of appeasement and carefully scripted lies, adopted ever since Moses told Miriam that Pharaoh wholly agreed to the idea of letting his people go!

My mother, of course, inspired more fear than any Pharaoh.

Chapter 2

The Bee on the Bimah

On one Sukkot, the women were granted the privilege of sitting amongst the men, in the downstairs section of the Shul. How woke of the late-nineties, Southampton Jewish males! Normally, the women would be forced to sit upstairs, looking down on the rest of those fortunate enough to be born with a penis, farther away from the Torah and prayer rituals, unable to participate or contribute, other than to bring post-prayer cakes on demand. On this particular occasion, it was deemed fit that all genders should sit together – something the males of the community came to quickly regret.

My father, the occasionally-paid Lay Cantor (prayer leader) of the Shul (synagogue), began the service as he had done for many years. As he benched (prayed), a light, buzzing noise could be intermittently heard from above. A bumblebee had found its way into the Shul, and was buzzing around the Bimah (raised prayer platform). My mother caught sight of the unsuspecting bee and quickly de-shoed.

The bee hovered above my father's head for a short time, in a fairly curious yet innocuous manner, eventually landing on the floor just by my father's feet. It was at this point that my mother sprang forth from her newly-established perch, and in one fell swoop battered the bee to death in front of the entire congregation.

And God!

The congregation stood agog, unable to quite fathom what had just happened. As my father prayed to the Lord Almighty, my mother had seen fit to kill one of His creations in front of His very eyes! Mid-prayer!

Still, this unprovoked, wanton attack did not faze my father, who continued with the service. My mother re-shoed and marched back to her pew, reopened her Sidur (prayer book) and pretended to read. The rest of us simply stared at her as she continued with her evening, unaware of the ridiculousness of her actions, having just battered a bee to death on a Bimah.

I'm sure she had good intentions; what if the bee had stung my father? How on Earth could this tiny provincial community have continued to pray and/or function in the future, with a stung Cantor?

Alas, the curious bee is no more. I can't remember how it was cleaned up, or whether the shoe, dead bee 'n' all, was simply placed back on my mother's foot.

So, in conclusion, in terms of inspiring fear to all creatures, great and small, my mum was a pound-for-pound champ!

I digress…

Chapter 3
Funeral Number One

My mum's funeral was an altogether eye-opening experience, a first for me, and an education in the ridiculousness of funereal ritual, and the somewhat comic attitude of attendees.

My dad chatted to his sister loudly and I shushed him, as he shushed me back. This comic, back-and-forth shushing continued for some time, until I could overhear him chitchatting about me.

Auntie Lis: "Lovely that Joey has found Rezanne – someone like her. Especially after what happened before."

Dad: "Mm, mm, his ex was a psycho!"

"She's lovely and he deserves her."

"Yes."

I agree with their sentiments, but maybe it was not the time and place to discuss my love life: whilst bent over my mother's grave!

Eventually, they took note of my disapproving stares and proceedings could continue. Telling off your own father for misbehaving at a graveside, whilst burying his partner of forty years, is an odd experience, to say the least.

After the dirt had been thrown and shovelled in my mum's general direction, my dad said a few words: a poem he had written for her. The congregation edged closer, step-by-step, to hear what they could of the poem. It was barely audible through my dad's mask and his perma-mumbled tone – nonetheless, you could feel the sentiment. The Anglo-Judaic diaspora spread themselves out between the headstones of the hedged-in Jewish cemetery, doing their best to hear the eulogy I had written and the poem that followed.

My dad always liked a poem. A very creative soul, he would often scrawl couplets on the back of National Trust leaflets. His pockets were always full of free leaflets, like the ones found in hotel foyers.

I stumbled through the *Mourner's Kaddish*, in broken, BarMitzvah-boy Hebrew. My brother remained silent. The rabbi passed us both transliterations before the service, which were harder to read than Hebrew, so I opted to battle through the backward hieroglyphs, with what I found to be a more able attempt than I expected.

We all dosey-doed to make space for one another, to exit the Jewish section of the Hollybrook Cemetery. Some attendees had kept more of a distance than others, more onlooker than mourner – albeit understandable, in the circumstances.

Before being allowed to leave, the rabbi led us through a kind of gauntlet of confused old Jews. He lined up those attempting to exit in parallel lines, and commanded that myself, my dad, my brother and Rezanne march down the middle. I have no idea as to the religious significance of the burial guard of honour we wandered into. My dad pushed and dragged his walking frame forward, but kept shuffling, at a 45-degree angle, toward the right side of the parallel human lines. Slowly, the right line edged backward, to maintain social distancing, and soon the lines descended into chaos, each Jew for themselves, as they scrambled to avoid contact with us and one another. After a period of madness, we reached the mouth – which was now the side of the tunnel – and made our way to the car park.

We dragged the shovel back to the car and threw it into the boot. The shovel, only briefly retired, would bury no more pets or people for a further six months.

*

At my dad's funeral, it was my turn to eulogize with a poem. Taking on the mantle of Davis-family-funeral poet, I did my best to struggle through, but I barely made it through each line. A mixture of tears and mask-muffled sounds, it probably didn't even make sense to those who braved infection, and were likely too far back to hear the words I managed to squeeze out between sobs:

"All That Remains"

All that remains is hurt and pain,
An empty void, a constant strain.
My heart is missing the part you took.
I missed you leave – an unfinished book.

The sky is empty now; they stole the stars,
And all that remains has left its scars.
I'm numb, Dad, I want you back.
Nothing can replace what I now lack."

All that remains are empty rooms and broken parts,
Empty plates, empty tables, empty chairs and empty hearts.
Paint me a picture, Dad, show me one last time,
Give me a piece of you, something I can call mine.

Please come back. I have no more tears to cry,
There's nothing left and my eyes are dry.

All that remains of the life you had.
I miss you, Mum. I miss you, Dad.

Rezanne rubbed my back throughout, hoping to quell the hurt. My brother stood silently, a masked statue bent over the graveside.

The lump in my throat choked me into silence.

Chapter 4

The Fancy-Goods Dealer

The initial shock of day one had passed. It was followed by a day of agitation and uneasiness.

Phone call after phone call, I felt like my dead mother's secretary. My brother, my wife and I all wandered from room to room, sifting through what remained of my mum's existence. The stench of sickness lingered, hanging in the air around the hospital bed, which had been moved into the living room at the moment she could no longer make it to the stairlift and up to her bedroom.

My father was planted firmly within the stench, his own indistinguishable from that which my mother had left behind. He had refused to shower or bathe in what had to be close to a year. His skin was so dry it began to flake off him, in scalelike chunks.

We moved upstairs, to search for those documents my mother had hidden away for the event of her death. She had scattered them about the house, rather than sensibly keeping all the paperwork together. It was now a post-mortem scavenger hunt to piece together her finances, will, personal belongings and anything else that needed to be done; it now lay scattered throughout the mess they had amassed, over forty years of senseless hoarding.

My mother came from a poor, Jewish immigrant family, her father having travelled to the U.K. from Chernovitz in modernday Ukraine (then the far-eastern end of the Austro-Hungarian Empire) as a young man, eventually settling in London and working as a "Fancy Goods Dealer". We only discovered this fact when we stumbled upon our grandfather's identity document, whilst clearing out my mother's belongings.

Sadly, my research into the family history has led me to understand that at least thirty-six Trichters were killed in the holocaust, over a hundred being listed on Yad Vashem's Shoah Database. As such, it is wholly possible that many of the family John Trichter left behind were victims of the holocaust.

Clearing what was left of my mother's worldly possessions proved to be equal parts sorrow, horror and sometimes simply confusion. Perhaps my least favourite find was the nude photos my father had taken of my mother, in some artistic photoshoot, whilst in their pre-child, black-and-white-erotica days. Every time I stumbled on one, scarred and scared by the image of one's mother erotically posing for their father, I would find another, then another. It started to feel like they were left for us to find, to prove a point, or simply my mother's last twisted attempt at pissing me off – something she enjoyed more than life itself. Some kind of posthumous Oedipal revenge for having dared to challenge her throughout my life.

Birth-control pills from the sixties; bottles of whisky, at the back of wardrobes for twenty years; baby teeth; eighties porn magazines; hundreds of bags of pound coins (now outdated); tombola prizes with the paper numbers still taped to them; a Berber dagger; Christmas cards from dead people; letters from dead people; pictures of dead people; a diary of sorts…

The diary included pages and pages of typed accounts of the feelings of isolation and disdain she felt for us. This quasijournal contained endless lists of fantastical accusations of belittlement and hurt, allegedly perpetrated by my brother and I as children, toward her. I read through all I could handle of the twenty-plus-year-old indictment. It was bizarre. She used to lock herself away from us daily, stewing and resenting, culminating in a fiction of what she must have felt justified her attitude toward the wider world: estrangement.

Her father died when she was very young, and I think from then on she resented the world. Further entries were more historical, talking of her childhood in the post-war East End, and how her richer family looked down on her and her poorer parents. She talked of hand-me-downs and tenement housing. Of her father's diabetes, and having to practice on an orange, in order to perfect the art of injecting him with his insulin.

Forced to grow up young, forced to feel inferior to others, and forced to care for a partially-blind mother, following her father's death, it's not hard to see why she hid away. Why she created a world where it felt okay to exist.

I didn't like my mother – in fact, I strongly disliked her the majority of the time. I loved her, I guess. When she died, it hurt the way it would hurt when someone you love dies, but I don't ever remember feeling like I loved her when she was alive.

Perhaps I was sad out of guilt for not feeling sadder, which had the predictable effect of providing me with the illusion of genuine sadness. It's hard to gauge and question whether I actually loved my mother. I did everything to try to please her – or, perhaps, appease her; I forget the difference sometimes.

We piled what could be of financial or emotional value in one dusty corner of the room, and continued to sieve through the remnants of her life.

Eventually, we stumbled on a leather envelope, filled with dozens of black-and-white photos of relatives and one colour photo: my half-sister, Leora. A letter from her mother, my father's ex-wife, sat beside it. A Rhodesian stamp straddled the corner of the 45-year-old envelope, dated 1975.

Chapter 5

Leora

I have discovered, over time, that old people keep secrets. They keep the past bottled up, hidden away in the deepest, darkest recesses of their psyches, so as not to admit to fault, shame or simply being human.

The truth is that my father abandoned his sick daughter, running away from responsibility when she was no older than seven. She died in 2017, having never seen her/our father again.

Following art school, my father followed his then-girlfriend to Rhodesia (now Zimbabwe). At some point early on, in the sixties, she left him for God and Jesus, choosing to become a missionary in Africa. Falling back on his Jewish roots, my father became involved with the Jewish Community in Salisbury (now Harare), and met Mischel, his first wife. They had one daughter: Leora.

In the early sixties, Leora contracted meningitis and suffered irreparable damage to her brain. She became deaf, and her cognitive development failed to develop beyond that of a young child, with an I.Q. of 70 well into her teens.

Their relationship became strained, as any would. My aunt recounted receiving very distressing letters about how bad things had become between them, culminating in violence. Eventually, my father had an affair with a Zimbabwean woman, and the relationship was more or less at an end. My grandmother booked a flight and headed out to Africa, to bring my dad home. He packed a bag, as if going to work on any normal day, and left for the U.K., never to return.

Maybe he said goodbye to his daughter, maybe he didn't – no one is left alive to tell me, either way.

I contacted the care facility I found in an old address book of my mother's. A local lady answered, with a thick Zimbabwean accent. She didn't know of a Leora Davis. She asked her colleague, who didn't know her either. I decided it best to contact the head office; maybe they would have some record of her. Maybe they would know if she was still alive.

In a day, I had done more to contact Leora than my father had in sixty years! Fuelled by embarrassment at my father's actions, or maybe even contempt for them, I eventually found someone able to help. He told me that Leora had sadly passed, in 2017. After prying, it became clear that she had died of a pulmonary embolism, but had been cared for by this organization for the majority of her adult life.

Then came the requests for money.

"Mr. Davis, your sister was cared for with limited government funding. The full amount outstanding for her care is 12.6 million Rand."

12.6 MILLION RAND!?

I had only been curious about what had happened to my sister, and had come out of it with a bill for a sum which could mean fifty million pounds or ten pounds, for all I knew!

After a quick Google conversion, I was able to surmise that the bill was roughly £200,000.

Chapter 6

The Rosovskys

The story goes that my great-grandparents on my father's side had taken a boat from Odessa, destined for a new life in New York. My great-grandmother was pregnant with my grandfather, Ninman, at the time. He was always known as Norman, and his real name only came to light after my brother and I cleared out my parents' filing cabinet; his Will was entitled: *Last Will and Testament of Ninman Davis.*

Rosen and Elisheva Rosovsky had bought tickets to New York, chasing the dream of a new start in a less anti-Semitic, pogromy world. The ship docked in the harbour, after a number of days at sea, and they disembarked, walking along the gangway with all of their worldly possessions in tow, making their way to what they believed to be Ellis Island's arrivals. No doubt confused and disoriented by the long voyage, they likely didn't think much of not having seen the Statue of Liberty or the tall skyscrapers of the NYC skyline.

The ship's passengers filed out, one by one, toward a new life in New York, and into the makeshift tents set up for the immigrants on arrival.

"Welchumm. Name?"

Rosen knew enough English to understand the request and respond: "Rosovsky."

"Ey? Wha?"

"Rosovsky"

"Mayt, lychh, what are yer sayin'?"

Rosen reacted quickly; he realized that he might have to Anglicise his name to some extent. He had heard from others, who had made similar journeys, that they'd had to change their names to assimilate on arrival, but they could still retain their name later on.

"David Rosovsky." David was a strong Jewish, yet easyenough-to-pronounce name, he thought. "David," he repeated.

"Wot, mayt? Okay, Davis? Your name is Davis?"

"Yes, David," responded Rosen.

Clearly misunderstanding the mistake that would affect generations to come.

Documents were endorsed and handed over to Rosen, and Dave and Ellie walked into their new home, with new names and new lives to live – in New York…?

The bleak skyline and odd accents were in stark contrast to the postcards and photos they had seen of the Big Apple.

The ship's horn blasted out as it sailed off.

All around them, bemused Russians fumbled about with their bags and children. Yiddish voices echoed around them:

"Vi zenen mir?" ("Where are we?")

"Iz das Niu Yark?" ("Is this New York?")

Sentiments of similar bemusement sounded out amongst the passengers, as they traipsed through the desolate dockland. Dockworkers went about their business around Rosen.

Where was he? This didn't feel like America. Had they been at sea enough time to have sailed across the entire Atlantic?

"Ekskuze mi, sir, ver are ve?"

"Mayt, this is Liverpoooool," barked one of the hurried dockworkers, unimpressed with the seeming stupidity of the question.

Liverpool?! Was this a mistake? They had paid for tickets to New York. These turn-of-the-20th-century people traffickers had swindled them!

And so, David and Eleanor Davis began their new lives as Liverpudlians.

Norman (nee Ninman) was born the following year: 1901 – the first British-born Davis. By happenstance, all future generations of Davis would be British, not American. My

Britishness can more or less be solely attributed to my greatgrandad being conned by a bunch of Scouse sailors, circa 1901.

Their names would be lost, their identities hidden, in attempts to assimilate and simply be understood.

*

My mum was a Trichter, not a Davis. Despite having told my brother and I that she and my father were married; they weren't and never were. I was around twenty when I rumbled their ruse.

My dad's name is David Davis, not Barry. David is his middle name.

My grandad was Ninman, not Norman.

My grandma was Gertrude, not Miriam (as she was known).

My great-grandfather was Rosen, not David (I'm not sure about my great-grandmother; Eleanor, rather than Elisheva, was more poetic licence than fact, but I'm sure that wasn't too far from the truth).

My dad had a secret family in Zimbabwe, then Rhodesia, which I found out about later, in mid-childhood.

Although my whole family history is… well, somewhat muddled with untruths and half-truths, and… well, some outright lies, I'm okay with it.

I might yet take back ownership of the Rokosovsky name, in some form. Hand it down to my children-to-be as a middle name, just to spark some confusion amongst all who try to pronounce it. We'll see.

Chapter 7

Day Three: Arrangements

Jewish funerals are fairly minimalistic events, more to do with ritual than fanfare. Of course, given my very much lapsed Jewishness, I was ill-prepared, to say the least, when it came to the rituals surrounding Judaic burials. Add to the mix the rituals Covid brought to the table, then you have a hotchpotch of nonsensical (to me) religious practices and nonsensical (to everyone) government guidance.

For a start, the number of people allowed at the graveside varies between what the government allow, what your local council allow, what your Beth Din (the organization that governs Jewish law and practices) allow, and what your rabbi is willing to accommodate, in light of all of the aforementioned. The result is… a mess.

Also, social distancing is a concept rather than guidance for my elderly relatives. My father believed the virus to be a government hoax until he died from it. My mother was too far gone to truly understand its significance.

I called the rabbi on the Monday, to finalize funeral arrangements. I was asked if I would like to do *Kriah*, the ripping of clothes. This ancient tradition is where the mourners (usually immediate family members) rip, tear or cut a piece of their clothing, or a ribbon attached to their clothing, to signify their pain, grief and hurt at the loss of a loved one.

"I'm sorry," I said, "my Jewish education is limited to Bar-Mitzvah-boy level; you'll have to explain to me what Kriah is."

"Aye, yoo reep a peese of ya clow-thin to seegnafay grrreeef," replied the Scotch rabbi.

I politely declined the offer.

Retorting with an alternative, he suggested: "Do yous have a bayygal an da boiled ayg? Yer farther, bruther and you need tweet a bayygal an da boiled ayg; it seegnafays lyfe. A bayygal an dan ayg – thair roond!"

It made sense: they are round, and I guess life is a kind of vicious circle – although I'm sure he meant it as a nice kind of symbolism, opposed to the recurring cycle of shite I took it to mean, in my cheerless state of mind.

"Yes," I responded, "I can make sure we can have a bagel and a boiled egg after the funeral."

"Thayn maymbers of thee comyunitee wish ye a lowng life".

We had planned to bury my mum on the Wednesday, her having died on the Saturday. Saturday until Wednesday is a huge amount of time to wait, in Jewish circles; many ultraorthodox Jews will bury the dead the day after their death. How they can manage this, I don't know; they must be forging death certificates and bribing cemetery and council staff, to facilitate such a queue-jump burial. I had no idea how much was involved, from registering the death to a doctor certifying the death, burial plots, funeral directors, rabbis, attendees and etc., etc., etc. The list goes on!

Chapter 8

Mum

My mum was who she was. Brought up sharing a tenement house in post-war East London, with a partially-blind mother and a diabetic father, who died by the time she was ten, she didn't have it easy.

She developed this habit of staring through people, into their very souls, to the extent that the level of discomfort was so palpable it often inspired violent reactions from people.

I can vividly recall one occasion, in The Marlands Shopping Centre in Southampton, when my brother and I were around maybe eight and ten. The Marlands is now home to about five different versions of Poundland, but at the time it was the place to be seen in Southampton – until the dawn of West Quay Shopping Centre, that is. The Marlands is now a glorified walkway through to the high street.

On this particular occasion, my mum, for some unknown reason, started staring at a man walking past us. Eyes fixed on him, she gave him the Linda stare, daring him to bite. She was the alpha in this shopping centre; who dared challenge Linda Davis/Trichter?

Unfortunately, on this particular occasion, he dared!

He began marching toward us, shouting at the top of his voice: "What the fuck do you think you're staring at? Stop fucking staring at me, you crazy woman! What the fuck do you want?!"

Her stare was unerring, unfaltering and wholly unnecessary; she stood her ground, protecting her young from the likely drunk passer-by. He continued his approach, but Linda had a plan! Out of her handbag, she pulled a rape alarm and yanked the cord.

Piercing through the centre and echoing up the escalators, all attention was drawn to my mum (and us), as she proceeded to shout back amidst the shrill siren of the Betterware catalogue-bought rape alarm.

A schoolfriend wandered past the scene with parents, judgingly sauntering past us. That Monday, at school, we would become the children of the mad woman in The Marlands.

Eventually, security descended upon the scene, doing their best to calm the man and to stop my mum from creating any more of a scene – which appeared impossible, given her intransigence and unparalleled belief in her own righteousness, when in the presence of the children. I can safely say that myself and my brother did not appreciate being used as a tool to justify her irrational behaviour, in this scenario or others.

The rape alarm silenced itself – through lack of battery, I imagine – but the shouting continued for a period, before the man relented. My mum stood, chest puffed out, daring others to stare. This was her domain!

My mum was not exactly a people person – as the above demonstrates.

The staring wasn't solely reserved for unsuspecting strangers; it was her weapon of choice against relatives, girlfriends, shop assistants, barbers, traffic wardens... well, anyone, to be honest.

When she first met my wife, Rezanne, she stared at her for a solid five minutes. Her judgement stare was finally broken by the words: "Do you love my son?"

"He's okay, I guess," replied Rezanne.

Wrong answer. Stare to continue until more satisfactory answer received.

Of course, there is also the "chair turn", an alternative to the more blatant show of disapproval of the stare. If she didn't like someone, or what they were saying, she would simply turn her chair away from them, so that she was facing the opposite direction to them – even if this meant that she was facing away from the group entirely.

On one occasion, around four years ago, we took my dad to lunch for his eighty-somethingth birthday, in Strada on Southbank. After eating, we took a short walk and then ended up in the café area of the Southbank Centre. My aunt (Dad's sister) joined us. Lis and Linda did not get along.

We were all chatting away, laughing about this and that, when my mum, noticing we were enjoying ourselves in conversation with Lis, decided to turn her chair in the middle of the conversation, and face herself in the complete opposite direction to the rest of us.

I prefer this to the arbitrary use of rape alarms, but it's on a similar level of anti-social behaviour.

Chapter 9

Nothing Leads to Nothing

"Nothing leads to nothing." My father muttered these words to himself as he slumped in his bottle-green, piss-soaked sofa. He was losing any sense of belonging in this world. It was quite evident that he was finding life too hard. Not necessarily finding it too hard without my mother (if anything, he found that element of the experience strangely liberating); he was finding the cumulation of ailments too much to cope with. "Nothing leads to nothing" was his profound way of poetically disguising the anguish of having nothing left; and where exactly that would lead him.

Mind you, it wasn't all doom and gloom: Barry had found freedom in his newfound bachelorhood. He proclaimed that my brother and I should find him a Polish girl, to take care of him. She could be his girlfriend and, in exchange, she could stay in the house for free.

At this point in time, my father had a catheter and a bag of wee more or less permanently attached to his leg, at all times. Nonetheless, that did not dissuade his efforts; he was adamant.

He saw himself as quite the catch. *"Elderly bachelor seeks live-in carer/lover/chauffeur to cook, clean, drive around, change catheter, clean up cat poo, clean up own poo (on occasion), shop, administer medication x100, and other household tasks. If interested, please contact Barry."* The phone would have been ringing off the hook!

But, who was I to shoot down his dreams of another chance at love? He had weathered Storm Linda[1] for forty years or so, so let the old man have his fun, I guess.

The fixation on an Eastern European girlfriend-carer continued for some months to come. Eventually, he settled on a middle ground: me visiting him more often. Was that what he wanted all along? To make me realize how lonely he was, by threatening to fritter our inheritance away on a Warsaw wedding? I doubt it; I think he genuinely thought that now was as good a time as any to have a quick fling. One last hurrah!

Sadly, nothing did lead to nothing. He slowly faded and then quite quickly passed. He never had the chance for one last hurrah… and I never really got to say goodbye.

---

[1] The name Linda has been used for eleven tropical cyclones worldwide. Hurricane Linda (1997; category-5) became the second-most intense hurricane in the Eastern Pacific basin, with a minimum pressure of 902 mbar, and the secondstrongest hurricane in the Pacific, in terms of sustained winds.
https://en.wikipedia.org › wiki › Tropical_Storm_Linda

Chapter 10

The Move

Removing my father from the indentation he inhabited within his living room was going to be no mean feat. It had got to the stage where things were growing from the outside in, slowly crawling their way toward Barry. Unwilling to let him go, plants were growing through the cracks in the outer wall, from the front garden, and had made their way into the living room itself, wrapping themselves around windowsills and resting patiently by Barry's side.

Triffids aside, simply brokering an agreement whereby the terms were such that he would agree to his reluctant removal would take some months. After a series of tactics, varying from bribery to coercion, trickery and threats of cat-napping, he eventually gave in, and it was agreed that he would be moved to a supported accommodation in Cardiff, where we could see him more frequently and care for him more effectively.

The family home would be uninhabited for the first time in forty years.

The carpet could take a break from its role as makeshift cat litter and occasional piss sponge, as my father decided to frequently pull apart his catheter, meaning that all it acted as was a tube from source to floor, bypassing the bag altogether.

The carers had long abandoned trying to argue with him about his personal hygiene, and wholly refused to assist with Poppy (the cat). "We don't gairt paid for thaaat," Sue the carer said, in a thick, Hampshire-hog twang, whilst plonking down a stale-looking corned beef sandwich on the coffee table.

My dad would now move onto his next dirty protest, within his own home. Poppy would not follow. We lied to my dad, saying it was "no pets allowed" at his new luxury accommodation. The truth was that he couldn't care for her, and we couldn't spend all of our free time cleaning up her mess. Nate took over the responsibility of caring for her, in secret (as he, in fact, wasn't allowed pets in his flat), until she could be rehomed.

Poppy and Barry were kindred spirits, ever-present in the indentation sunk deep in the bottle-green sofa – him slumped, eyes fixed on Sky Sports; her curled up tightly on his lap, refusing to move, claws ready to grab onto his trousers to prevent removal, if it was ever foolishly attempted.

She died a week after we moved dad to Cardiff. We never told him.

We packed my car (well, my dad's car, but he had been banned from driving after the G.P.'s receptionist followed him home from the surgery, only to find him arbitrarily pulling out into oncoming traffic at every opportunity), and set off for what my dad would come to call his "very comfortable cage".

Chapter 11

T-Rex Rabbit

My dad was an extremely gifted artist, having exhibited his artwork throughout his career, and having worked as a secondary school art teacher and graphic designer in his younger years.

Unfortunately, in later life his art had become quite… different. His previously well-crafted sketches and paintings had given way to a series of pen-and-ink scratchings, spending hours on end scrawling black scribbles over whatever paper was closest to his wee-soaked throne.

The finest of these scribble masterworks was "T-Rex Rabbit", named by the artist. It involved an abstract depiction of a dinosaur (most likely a T-Rex) arching over a rabbit by his feet. What on Earth inspired him to immortalize these two creatures together I don't know, but it was likely indicative of his gradual lack of grip on reality, which was slowly slipping away.

He couldn't remember all that much anymore, and was finding it particularly hard to concentrate on what was going on around him. Being in large groups of people was especially difficult.

However, on the flip side, complete isolation and lack of stimulus appeared to have similar effects.

He'd always had a loose grip on sanity, and now he was slowly releasing his grip on lucidity. His art had always been the litmus test for his state of mind. If he was struggling, he couldn't paint; couldn't express himself. Everything became very dark.

Dad: "Joey, what do you think of this?"

Me: "What is it, Dad?"

Dad: "It's a crow man."

Me: "What?"

Dad: "See? It's a crow and it's a man."

Me: "It's no 'T-Rex Rabbit', Dad."

"Crow Man" was just one of his many latter creations.

T-Rex Rabbit has now been rehomed with a lovely family, and is living a new life with one of Rezanne's colleagues. She loves it! Lord knows why; it's truly disturbing.

His poetry – well, actually, his illustrated poetry booklets – was meticulously self-published, using an HP Inkjet photocopier, Pritt Stick and a black Berol ink pen. Among his mature works were *Poems of War and Violence* and *Poems of Dismay* (and others). Everything was quite morose, whether it be his artwork or his writing. It was all taking a darker turn.

To illustrate this dark turn, I have taken an extract from one of his poems, "The Girls of Holy Cross":

"The Girls of Holy Cross."

"Hate-filled houses spill their venom "Onto
unsuspecting streets.
"A barrage of petrol bombs smash cars.
"Inflamed passions pour acid onto bonnets…"

It continues in the same vein.

Or, perhaps, his most to-the-point, latter work, "Death":

"Death."

"Death is the absence of life, or is life the absence of death?
"The reality creates revulsion not many can tolerate.
"The decay, the gradual rotting of flesh nauseates.
"We enclose the corpse in a box and pay homage to life."

"Innocence Murdered", "The Oven", "Requiem (Death in Portswood)"… the list goes on; visceral morbidity mixed in with some simply depressive prose. There's a 22-page, illustrated, handmade book of these. And there's another booklet, almost as many pages long, similarly illustrated.

They may be painfully depressing in content and subject matter, but they were so articulate and lucid, for someone who most days struggled to function as a human being, other than to watch Sky Sports and pet the cat.

He read a poem at my mum's funeral which was actually beautiful. He wrote it that morning and read it that afternoon, whilst Rezanne, my brother and I stared at him in disbelief. *How the hell did he write that?* Our silent eyes whispered to each other the same confused statement.

At this stage, he had been diagnosed with mild cognitive impairment (M.C.I.), the early stages of dementia. So, seeing him able to collect his thoughts in such a lucid fashion was quite reassuring, albeit confusing. Like he was putting it on, to receive more cups of tea without having to get up himself. This was increasingly likely: he didn't have dementia, he just didn't want to make his own tea, as that involved getting up.

Chapter 12

Cardiff

We packed Dad's Kia Picanto to the brim with the many belongings he refused to part with. Anything else he needed we could get to him later, we promised. A very white lie! We had hoped that he would forget about everything he had hoarded over the years, once he saw what a non-crap-filled space could look like.

The thing we failed to grasp is that he truly enjoyed living in his own filth. He had absolutely no desire to be clean; in fact, he wanted to be dirty. Refusing to bathe, like a petulant child, he wriggled and writhed as I frantically attempted to flannel him down, whilst spraying as much water at his body as I could, before he would inevitably decide he'd had enough of being militarily hosed down whilst straddling his bath seat.

We set off for pastures new, car full of crap and now smelling like it. Wee slowly leaked out of the catheter, into his socks and shoes, drip by drip. I tightened and emptied it, but he found a way to fiddle with it every minute or two, to the extent that it might as well just have been an open tube flooding urine out through a trouser-camouflaged left leg. Marking his territory like a dog with a cocked leg, he leaked his mark throughout doctors' surgeries and supermarkets, his and others' cars, and taxis throughout the Greater Southampton area. Now he was off to South Wales to do the same.

Head held high, he didn't look back at the chaotic ruin that was 42 Ripstone Gardens, his home of close to forty years. Clawing at the space where the seatbelt was, he was unable to manoeuvre his body to pull it across for himself. I leant across, pulled it over and strapped him in. And off we went! No pitstops required: his toilet was attached to his leg.

*

He lasted one day before he pulled the emergency cord, a further six hours before he pulled it again, one week at the accommodation before he was taken to hospital, and two weeks before he died of Covid.

His stint at Cwrt Brynteg was short-lived, and his new Welsh life equally so.

*

I left his flat at around nine p.m., having freshly microwaved a cottage pie for him, and placed it on the coffee table in front of him to eat. Shortly before dinner, I had tried to sit him at the dinner table, but he proceeded to spill a pint of orange juice over the entirety of the table and all over the carpet below.

I was exhausted. I had brought him closer to provide muchneeded support, and to give him a better quality of life, but I had become his carer/parent.

This parent-child role reversal began at the point my mum died. He had regressed to a state of complete reliance upon others, in order to function day-to-day.

At around ten p.m., I had a call from the manager of the supported accommodation.

"Your dad has been found wandering the streets. He was looking for you. You need to reassess how suitable he is for this type of accommodation. I've had to come to the property out of hours to take care of this."

Not an ounce of empathy in his voice. How someone with such disdain for his duties could end up in a role which requires such a degree of understanding, I will never know.

When I messaged him a couple of days later, to let him know that my dad had Covid, and he had been in close contact so would likely need to isolate, his response was: "Well, that's ruined my Christmas, then!" He never asked if one of the residents under his care was alive or dead, well or unwell. Simply concerned about consumption of turkey and the opening of presents, his embittered, selfish response reverberates throughout my recollection of Dad's relocation to Cardiff.

A true scumbag!

I emptied my dad's belongings from the flat, handed back the keys and did all of the paperwork, with not a word from him.

When I arrived at the flat, an ambulance was parked up on the hilled drive. An Ocado delivery driver had apparently spotted my dad sat on the floor of the road, waving down traffic.

"Where do you need to go?" the driver had asked.

"My son – Portswood." (The area in Southampton where we had lived.)

Somehow, the Ocado driver had led or transported him to the supported accommodation. I imagine he put two and two together and realized what might have happened. He helped him to his feet and took him back to the accommodation, calling an ambulance along the way.

Dad went looking for me. I had told him: "I'll see you soon, Dad. I have to go home now." Then I closed the back door and drove off...

...returning no more than an hour or two later, to find him in an ambulance.

"What happened, Dad?"

Rezanne held his hand within her left hand, stroking it with the right.

"I don't know. Where did you go?"

"I told you, Dad, that I was going home. Don't you remember?"

He stared absently into the back of the ambulance. I stroked his hair, trying to calm him and make him feel at ease.

The paramedics quizzed me about his medical history, and I explained that I would take care of him and that he could leave the ambulance; no need to take him to hospital. This was a ridiculous suggestion, but I just panicked, and didn't want him to go into a hospital full of Covid cases. The paramedics told me they would have to take him in for a check-up, just as a bare minimum.

I wasn't allowed to come with him, due to the current Covid restrictions in place; I would have to call the hospital for an update. So, Rezanne and I said our goodbyes, reassuring him that it was just a check-up, and that we would see him as soon as we could. I told him that I loved him and off he went.

That was the last time I saw him conscious.

We locked up the flat and headed home.

He was safer at the hospital, wasn't he? He could be cared for there – right? He wouldn't go walking off into the night, looking for me there – surely? All these questions swam through my head, bouncing off the sides as I drove us back to our flat.

The following day, I was called with the update that he had Covid. He would be moved to a Covid ward.

That was where he would live out his last days.

In fact, when he was first tested he was asymptomatic. They didn't even treat him for the virus. It was around ten days later that things took a turn for the worse.

His carer on the ward, Gali, had been the facilitator of contact between us. As my dad couldn't use a phone very well, if at all, at this point in time, he helped us to Facetime him. We managed a couple of blurry calls, shouting down the phone that we loved him and we would see him soon.

I don't remember his last conscious words to me. I don't remember anything, other than the call that followed. Anything earlier has been superseded by the weight of the intolerable pain we witnessed in the call that would follow.

"The doctors have left him!" Gali screamed down the phone. "I shouldn't be making this call, but you need to know so that you can do something. They've left him alone and moved him away from all of the other patients – and I don't know what to do!"

My dad was rolling around his bed, screaming, his eyes rolling into the back of his head, his hands rigidly held against the sides of his head in a Munchian scream. He barked and screamed and wailed, completely out of touch with reality, writhing about his bed as Gali tried to calm him.

There was nothing anyone could do; the virus had resulted in a secondary encephalitic/meningococcal infection and travelled to his brain.

That call, those screams, will never leave me until the day I die. His pain echoes in me every time I think of him. I think of how lonely he must have been, as the pain escalated and became so unbearable. I can't forgive myself for not being with him and holding his hand, even if I couldn't have done anything to change it… even if I wasn't allowed to be by his side. Nothing can remove the guilt or anguish that call has left in my heart.

I feel hollow every time I think back.

His pain took a part of me away that I can't get back. Not an innocence, or some kind of purity; it took part of my soul, and left it blackened and empty. I do my best to push away the thoughts and pacify myself, but I can't close my eyes to it; there is a void in me, a chasm of hurt that will never be filled. Rather, it will linger there, the scarred tissue of grief, never quite the same as before, always ever-so-grey and discoloured from the pain that left it there.

Chapter 13
Mad Dogs and Englishmen

My dad wasn't a well man, having struggled with his mental health since he was a teenager, his first mental breakdown having been when he was around 19/20 years old. That's pretty young by anyone's standards. It's therefore fair to say he was troubled.

During my childhood, he had two further mental breakdowns, resulting in him being sectioned for close to a year when I was nine, and several months when I was sixteen. He was a manic depressive, as it was known at the time – now more commonly known as bipolar disorder.

It began for me at Marchwood Priory Hospital.

From the outside, the priory was an idyllic and tranquil retreat. A whitewashed Georgian façade belied the pain within its walls. A grand piano sat in the communal room, which my dad would often play, entertaining the priory's guests and lessso-guests. Unable to deal with being a secondary school art teacher, he was wholly able to recall the entirety of a Tchaikovsky piano concerto.

I don't remember much about his descent into his detachment from reality. I know it felt sudden and, for a young child, quite confusing and distressing in equal measure. His first breakdown during my lifetime appeared to have been caused by a combination of the loss of his father and the inability to deal with the stresses associated with secondary school teaching – the confusion for me always being that he was an art teacher; how stressful could that be? Anyway, artists are tortured souls, forever striving for inspiration – so we'll leave it at that. Perhaps he strove for a muse within his own anguish; who knows?

It's quite difficult to truly distinguish between the memories that are real and the ones where I have filled in the gaps – or "false memories", as I believe they are known. I have pieced together in my mind the fading fragments from twenty-seven years of recall, and tried to create some semblance of what I would call a "clear recollection", but the truth is that there is no difference between what is real or a false memory, as I have no way to differentiate between the two.

I remember him screaming down the hallways and shaking uncontrollably, whilst muttering to himself inaudibly. I remember that he smelled different, the way sick people smell when they haven't washed for an undefined period of time: stale urine on stale clothes; unwashed skin and greasy hair.

I remember the E.C.T. – or electroconvulsive therapy. During E.C.T., an electric current is passed through the brain, creating a small seizure, in order to treat mental disorders.

Essentially, they fry your brain ever so slightly, so that you forget why you felt bad.

When asked how he was doing, my dad would always answer: "Hmm, medium to well." Perhaps this was a vague reference to having been briefly fried. "Hmmm" was the way he would start nearly every sentence, the sound that would punctuate nearly every word, and the coda at the end of every statement. He mumbled a lot! Sometimes he more or less communicated in mumbles alone, not words.

"Tea, Barry?"

"Mmm."

"Sugar?"

"Mmm."

"What would you like for dinner?"

"Mmm-mmm."

Come to think of it, they were more growls than mumbles. Imagine chatting to a small bear, who could understand everything you said, and could speak but didn't fancy it, so therefore spoke to you with some kind of in-between, nasal growl. Picture that and you're there.

I say I remember the E.C.T., but I clearly only remember the aftermath: the hallways, the visits, his distant stares. He wasn't really the same after the treatment.

My father was distant, troubled.

Visits were infrequent. My mum didn't drive and we had to take the bus for an hour, to get from Highfield to Marchwood, Marchwood being a small country village in the New Forest, and Highfield being more or less central in Southampton. We would traipse ourselves over there, after school, in the rain and the dark, arriving on the side of an A-road in the New Forest. A seven-year-old, a nine-year-old and a fifty-nine-year-old sprinting across to the right-hand side of the road, toward the long, winding drive up toward the country house which contained all those lost souls. I can't remember how we ever got home. I can only assume we stood flagging down buses in "alder shfatz jaren" – what my mum would call "the middle of nowhere", in Yiddish. I looked this up, and those aren't the Yiddish words for this phrase; it should be: "in mitd in ergets nit." I have no idea what "alder shfatz jaren" actually means, but my mum would say it with surprising frequency, so it must mean something, or simply nothing at all.

Whenever we would come to visit in daylight hours, a black-and-white border collie would accompany us up the path, toward the main house, and occasionally play with us in the grounds beneath the large tree which stood at the entrance. Her name was Jay. She was from the farm which neighboured the priory, and would wander over when the day's work was done. We loved Jay. She was a distraction from all the madness (quite literally). She later became pregnant and we bought one of her puppies, whom we named Jason (son of Jay).

Quite clever, I thought, for a nine-year-old. Anyway, I was an idiot. This dog was mad: absolutely uncontrollable, untrainable and unimaginable.

Nonetheless, I loved Jason. He was my dog.

Things took a turn for the worse for my dad, and it became clear that his condition could not be managed within a nonsecure facility such as Marchwood, so he was moved to St. Ann's, in Poole. At least, that's how I remember it; he may have just wanted to move to Poole. I actually have no idea exactly why he moved; that's just the reason I chose to remember.

St. Ann's use of E.C.T. was far more frequent, and the effects more severe. His already worryingly loose grip on reality loosened further, and he slipped into varying degrees of catatonia, unwilling to engage with doctors, friends, other patients – and us. Sat in the grounds, he stooped, hunched over a bench, shaking back and forth, his left leg bouncing up and down in a state of furious agitation. My mother tried to coax out of him some form of conversation, parading my brother and I in front of him, in the hope it would ignite some awareness of his existence. He just continued to stare and shake.

The grounds of St. Ann's overlooked the sea, from a hilltop. The grounds were scattered with trees and green open space – strangely idyllic, but in stark contrast to the acrid hallways of the hospital itself. The unwashed shuffled in and out of rooms, as their smell and agitation followed them. A train of angst floated behind the residents, as they staggered in different directions, without any apparent purpose.

Not much of my father remained.

One evening, we received a call from the hospital. My mum perched on the stairs by the front door, the curled, light-green telephone wire stretched to its maximum. She seemed immediately agitated and was shouting down the phone – though, shouting wasn't indicative of anything; she shouted at the toaster. This went on for some time, until the phone was abruptly hung up.

"Your dad is missing," she said, tears in her eyes.

To an eight- or nine-year-old, this doesn't mean a great deal, as there's a limited amount of understood context. I remember thinking that he would be back soon; he's probably just popped out. Of course, he hadn't just popped out.

We frantically packed a few things and my mum made another call. We were going to head to a friend's house in Christchurch, to be closer to the hospital whilst they looked for him. I say "friend"; he was actually a patient from Marchwood, whom my parents had become close to during his time there. He was an alcoholic, but appeared outwardly to be a very functioning member of society.

We arrived at their house late at night and settled in the living room. My mum spent the majority of the evening on the phone to the hospital and the police. A manhunt ensued.

The police trawled the cliffside by the hospital, as my mum worried that he had wandered too far beyond the hospital grounds and fallen – or maybe fallen intentionally. The search continued throughout the night.

My brother and I stayed up late, running around their living room, setting up assault courses with pouffes and coffee tables, no one encouraging us to go to bed, no one paying us much mind. Gradually, we came to terms with the gravity of the situation, as everyone's emotions hung in the room. I think his name was John. His wife, also present, remains nameless as far as my memory is concerned.

I can't remember where or when we fell asleep, but I remember waking up to the hurried sounds of everyone adult rushing about, as phones rang and kettles boiled. He had been found!

Someone had found him at Poole Arts Centre, wandering outside. He had walked three miles, through the night, in search of art. Perhaps in search of some normality – who knows? I never asked him why he went there or whether it was planned. I presume it had to be planned. But, then again, he might have just walked and walked until he found something worth stopping for.

As I mentioned earlier, he was obsessed with leaflets. He would read them endlessly, devouring every word, from front to back. Model railways, pottery museums… maybe he had picked up a *"Visit Poole Arts Centre"* leaflet, which had been left behind by a visitor. Maybe he had one stuffed in a coat pocket, from his pre-hospital life. It's hard to say.

He was transported back to the hospital the following day. I like to think he was somewhat proud of himself, having escaped the grips of Dorset's version of Nurse Ratched, in a *One Flew Over the Cuckoo's Nest*-esque break for freedom. And that on the journey back he sat triumphant: Chief Barry, head held high, shake-free, a wry smile at having won this one small battle with his demons, and those demons forced upon him by the no-doubt-archaic mental-health treatment of the mid-nineties.

Some months later, he was released from section and returned home. He never returned to St. Ann's or Poole Arts Centre.

Chapter 14
The Ward

You would enter the Covid ward through the deserted concourse, where a solitary coffee shop braved the conditions, to peddle the worst lattés known to man, for those who had no other choice. Empty hallways wound toward the stairways and lifts which took you up to the ward.

I can't remember who told us how to get to the ward, or whether it was signposted; it feels like we just ended up there. As if the ward had its own gravitational pull on those who had the misfortune of having to enter, whether as patient, employee or family member. There are so many stress-blanks in my head that I simply have to fill in the gaps sometimes.

We entered a corridor covered in yellow-and-black tape, doors sealed shut, windows blacked out with tape, or signposted with warnings not to enter. This apocalyptic, Chernobyl-esque hospital wing was the Covid ward.

The corridors looped around the building until we ended up at what appeared to be the ward we had been directed to attend. We pushed our way through the yellow-taped double-doors.

One of the nurses shouted over to us: "You can't be here. What are you doing here?" We explained the situation and were passed whatever P.P.E. the NHS could muster: face mask, plastic face-shield, plastic gloves and a glorified bin bag, which appeared to be some kind of apron/bib.

Nurses faintly chattered outside of his room, their words muffled out by layers of surgical mask. It became a sort of faint hum, as each nurse shuffled past, buzzing about between the dying or not-so-dying patients of this particular Covid ward. Wires and cables bleeped and churned, as tubes drooped downward, whooshing air upward.

We walked into his room, ushered in by sympathetic nurses. They closed the door behind us, and we were left alone with what was outwardly my dad; whatever was left of him inwardly hung on in spirit, rather than in presence. His ghost lingered, waiting to say its goodbyes.

"Hi, Dad." The words barely made it out of my mouth; they fell out, one by one. Two syllables tempered with so much grief that they palpably weighed heavy on my tongue. I walked over to him, to the side of his bed closest to the window, whilst Rezanne sat to his left, with my brother perching at the foot of his hospital bed. Surrounded, he lay there beeping and whooshing, grasping at whatever oxygen filtered upward. The oxygen mask kept defiantly slipping off, held on by a shoelace-thin piece of elastic. He gargled and dragged at the air, then exhaled peacefully, rested for a second, before gasping and gargling all over again.

His hands were warm. Hot, in fact. It made him feel so… living. I held his hand and stroked his arm. I made myself believe that he was grasping my hand in return, but I know I was simply comforting myself with the lie of reciprocation.

He wasn't conscious. The virus had reached his brain and turned to encephalitis.

My face shield steamed up with hot breath and tears.

I pawed at my face with whatever part of my clothing I could push upward, to avoid touching my skin with those parts of me that had been exposed to the ward. In the end, it became a futile exercise. My eyes filled and stung, as I tried to blink out the tears without wiping them away, but I couldn't. I was blind, grasping away at my father's one hot hand.

He loved to hold hands, always a very tactile, loving dad. He would often hold Rezanne's hand for hours. And, if you pulled away, his vice-like grip would pull you back toward him. He had these unbelievably muscular hands, from playing the piano. Even as his age took its toll, his grip remained. Attempting to pry the remote from him, to turn the volume down from 100, would result in a fierce tug of war that he would always win.

My aunt recently drew a picture of him sat on his green, leather throne, cat on lap, Sky T.V.-remote in hand. Like a regal portrait, with a deerhound and a sceptre or rifle, Barry proudly sat slumped in his own wee (and maybe some of the cat's), with his remote in hand, ready to increase the volume to deafening levels, at the threat of any televisual intervention from those who dared to enter his domain.

Reclining Male with Cat and Remote Control, by Elisabeth VanDyk, 2021.

Barry was King of the Couch and Lord of the Lounge.

My aunt joked at his stone-setting, ten months later, that if Barry was to be reincarnated, he would come back as a remote control. Brilliant!

On one occasion, in 1985/86, he let me have the remote. I don't remember ever being allowed such a privilege again.

We sat by his side, reminiscing over his ridiculousness. It seems clichéd, but you fall naturally into a comforting reminiscence. Able to laugh at the worst of times. Laugh at the contents of his pockets: leaflets for cinema times from the nineties, or coupons for shops long since closed. Laugh at his obsession with beefburgers and corned beef. Most beef-based products became obsessions in later life, to the extent that there was an almost outright refusal to consume anything other than beef!

He dragged away at the air as we laughed or cried, or both. Sometimes we sat in silence for an hour or so, just thinking. My head swam with thoughts, regrets, plans, pangs of hurt and pre-emptive grief. It spun and swirled with uninterrupted blasts of everything.

I collected myself for a moment, to try to prioritize what we needed to do urgently. I went down to the concourse, to grab us coffees and call the funeral directors.

Caffeine and undertakers appeared the most obvious and pressing issues.

Their number was already saved on my phone from before: Head and Wheble Funeral Directors, the buriers of choice for the Southampton Hebrew Congregation, and much of the south coast Jewry.

By this point, I had already gone through the motions in July. Six months later, I was making the same phone call, albeit this one was pre-emptive (by about six hours) and involved an infectious disease. I didn't have the same panic and uncertainty as before, but nonetheless I stuttered and drew a blank as soon as I pressed the call button. I had given them pre-warning with my mum; enquiring about the process and explaining that she was terminally ill. With my dad it was different: it was sudden. Albeit I didn't expect him to survive much longer, in his state of health, I didn't expect him to go so soon.

How do you go about ordering the advance transportation of your father's body, whilst he's still alive? Would he lie there alone or be transported to some quarantined death-ward, where the bodies of the stricken lay uncollected. The pandemic's lost-luggage room flashed into my imagination: row upon row of the expired, who could not be touched until safe to do so. I didn't want this; I wasn't ready. They agreed to pick up the body as soon as they could get there, after he passed away.

"The body." The phrase, laced with anonymity, made me uncomfortable when it left my mouth.

"My father's body" made me feel even worse.

I choked back the tears as I hung up the phone. My throat felt like it was being dragged downward, through my body.

Arrangements were in place.

Coffee.

I walked back through the asbestos-chic, marginally-preThatcher wasteland. The strip-lights hummed along the corridors, until they appeared to darken as they met the entrance to the Covid ward. I pushed back through the yellow tape and replaced my old P.P.E. with new. Freshly wrapped, I took the sharp left into my father's room.

Rezanne and Nate hadn't moved. They chatted, about what I don't know or can't recall.

Rezanne's turn.

We alternated so that someone would always be there, in case something happened.

Rezanne returned with a cup of grey-looking tea, and was led to a windowless room in order to drink it, away from contamination. She returned not long after, and we continued the process of waiting for the inevitable.

Chapter 15

Aftermath (Nightmares and Suicide Attempts)

Firstly, before I continue with this chapter, I should add, for the more concerned readers; that the suicide attempt is not mine, nor anyone I know – just in case you were worried for my well-being… I'm sad, not suicidal.

No cause for concern here.

After my parents' deaths, the nightmares began.

I would wake up screaming during the night, seeing them in the room as if they were there, haunting me, following me around. Night after night, to the extent that I was genuinely afraid to go to sleep.

My parental ghosts lingered in my subconscious psyche alternately, never together. It was quite an orderly haunting that I experienced.

Every so often, I would be dreaming away quite peacefully, then one of them (usually my mum) would appear out of nowhere and give me the fright of my life.

This continued for months on end.

Eventually, I started to expect their appearance within my dreams, to the extent that it became a somewhat welcome haunting – a kind of subliminal reunion. It went from unbridled terror to melancholy, eventually transitioning toward a broad acceptance of their presence.

It sounds bizarre for an atheist to suggest that they believed in ghosts for a period, but I genuinely did.

I couldn't come to terms with the fact that I could be so psychologically affected, and that it could manifest itself to that degree of consistent, unrelenting haunt.

So, me and my ghosts met at night for some months, until their visits became less and less frequent.

Fading away into the darkness, my parents left me.

I miss it now, although the sheer fear I felt at the early stages of the haunting was something I wouldn't ever want anyone to experience. The more tolerable, latter stages I feel some nostalgia for. I felt comforted by their ghosts, and maybe, if ghosts are real (which I highly doubt), then maybe that was their desired effect all along. Maybe they were aware that I wasn't ready to let go and needed a bit more time with them; whether that might be supernatural or not, they felt my pain and tried to heal it.

Okay, at the start that did not work at all. I thought I would be haunted and traumatized forever, caught in the perpetual

P.T.S.D. cycle of losing two parents within six months. In the end, I had comfort. In the end, I had some semblance of… I don't know… solace, catharsis, peace… who knows? I just felt better. I missed them and they were there.

Ghosts linger in my thoughts rather than my subconscious now – peacefully remembering; a calming nostalgia. It appears that my ghosts finally rest in peace, content with the lives they led and all they left behind.

*

In the ten days that followed my father's death, we had to selfisolate, as was the protocol/law at the time. Of course, when you have lost someone so close to you, cooping yourself up in a small space, in quite painful grief, isn't beneficial to one's health.

A walk? An isolated, masked-up walk – what could that hurt? We won't come across anyone. We'll take the back paths, around the lake nearby. No one will even know we've left the house, and we will have some break from the solitude and confinement.

So, Rezanne and I quietly made our way downstairs and out of the flat. Sheepishly, we prised open the front door to the building, and snuck out into the wider world.

We tiptoed out of the front gate, only to hear some strange noises emanating from the block of flats more or less adjoining ours. We looked up to see a girl hanging out of the third-floor window to her flat. Half in, half out, she sat on the ledge, holding onto the window frame whilst making occasional sudden movements, as if she wasn't sure whether she was going to jump or head back into bed. Clothed in loosely-fitting PJs, she made wailing noises not so dissimilar to that which my dad made in the hospital, when we Facetimed him with Gali.

I tried to talk to her, attempting to engage in some conversation to make her feel more at ease.

By this point, some people had gathered to witness the spectacle. A limited number really attempted to help or do anything, other than socially distance themselves from one another and the drama, at this point.

"What's your name?" I called up. "Talk to me. It's okay. Maybe you should head back inside."

She didn't respond, simply stared blankly into the distance, rocking back and forth.

"What flat is she in?" Rezanne asked one of the other onlookers.

"Flat six," she said. "We've seen her around. I think she has mental health issues."

Rezanne gained entry to the apartment block and headed upstairs, to try to get inside her flat and pull her back in. I kept attempting to talk her off the ledge and placate her, but there was no response, other than more wailing.

"I think she's going to jump. We need to try to catch her if that happens. Has anyone called the police?" I shouted.

A man behind me nodded, and gestured to the phone by his ear.

At this point, a couple of other males joined me and we started to form a human circle of hands and arms, hoping this was just precautionary.

"She might just fall. I don't know," I said to the male to my left.

As soon as I said this, it happened: she jumped or fell – I don't know which, but she was on her way down… fast.

She clattered through my arms and the arms of the guy to my left, breaking our human net, and smashed into the guy to my right, landing fully on him.

Rezanne and another girl came running down. "What happened?"

No answer was required: they could see the aftermath. She lay prostate on the floor, half on the male that was to my right and half on the floor, still wailing.

Then the police arrived, as punctual as ever (the police station is less than one kilometre from where this took place, basically at the end of the street).

We covered her in blankets and the man-cum-landing pad explained what had happened, as I snuck off, hoping my Covid-isolation breach would remain unknown.

The moral of the story is clear: don't fuck with lockdown rules. If you do, people will fall on you from the sky!

On a serious note, this really is indicative of something far deeper in terms of what isolation can do to anyone, let alone those unfortunate enough to suffer with mental illness, isolating them when they need support most.

As she lay on the floor, her left breast had fallen out and one of her neighbours tucked it back in, covering her as best as she could, with whatever blankets us and others had managed to quickly muster in the panic. We don't know what became of her, but I hope she was given the support she needs.

Lockdown did a lot of different things to a lot of people.

I didn't leave the flat again until the ten days were up. I had learnt my lesson the hard way.

Chapter 16
The Twig

"The Twig" was a poem my dad wrote when he was a troubled teenager, about coming to terms with mortality and life's journey. It echoed his troubled mind, never fully feeling that he had a place in the world, perhaps, or not understanding it.

In the days that led up to my parents' stone-settings, I searched everywhere for "The Twig": every box, every bag of papers disregarded and yet to be sorted. I asked his sister, his poetry group, searched hard drives, old email accounts – nothing. "The Twig" was lost.

Perhaps aptly. My dad was the Twig, and once he had gone, the poem disappeared, too – like, when he died it actually simply floated off, into the ether, drifting down life's path until it was simply time. He'd had his good innings.

It had to be read at the stone-setting. It couldn't be lost. I had to do something: find it, replace it, rearrange the date until "The Twig" reappeared…

After much trepidation, I decided the only resolution was for me to write my own Twig. I knew the general idea of Dad's poem, and how it more or less ended. His was just so succinct – so right. My "The Twig" is an ode to his "The Twig".

I read his "The Twig" for a verse-speaking competition in school, when I was maybe thirteen. I didn't win – I think I came second or third – but it didn't matter; I loved that I read out something of his. I was proud that it came from him. I was proud that *I* came from him.

And so I wrote "The Twig (Revisited)". I read it out before friends and family, and choked back the tears, trying to distance myself from the reality of it all, so as to get through the entirety of the poem without becoming a blubbering mess.

I made it through.

"The Twig (Revisited)"

The twig was really quite everyday,
Quite non-descript, and somewhere between brown and grey.
To tell it apart from its fellows an onerous task,
Camouflaged amidst a sea of wind and bark.

Its leaves had fallen, its bark was frayed,
Bereft and unladen and partly decayed.
In Spring he had been quite something to behold,

Verdant, unburdened, its brown shining bold.

Though Autumn had left him quite underprepared...
    For the trials and tribulations, for which previously little he cared.
    The storm winds had torn him from the place he once called home.
    Left adrift below – all at once alone.

    So, off the twig drifted on untrodden path,
    Caught in a stream, meandering through wetland and marsh.
    He took one look back from where he had came,
    Drifting without purpose, recourse or even an aim.

    He pondered existence, his long, quite tangled past
    And accepted the current would take him at last.
    The river was strong and he needn't look back;
    He let it take him, accepting of a life that did not lack.

    Off out to sea – it was calm. The current did cease.
    Closed his eyes, breathed in. For now he was at peace.

The congregation et al drifted away from the gravesides, as I found a solitary twig in the bushes, toward the right of his grave, and gently placed it at the base of the headstone.

"'Bye, Dad," I whispered.

One day I will find "The Twig" – his Twig. I'll be sixty years old and it'll fall out of an old book of his. A makeshift bookmark will float to the ground and his Twig will be reborn. But, until then I will always remember; I won't forget him.

"The Twig" will be revisited.

'Bye, Dad… You had a good innings!

Chapter 17

Cakes in Tears

My mum circled the room, brandishing her famous apple cake, now heavily laced with the tears of disapproval. "Would you like some apple cake? I made it myself," she reiterated over and over, to anyone who would listen – occasionally breaking into a sob, in whatever part of the room had the most people, so as to draw enough attention to herself as humanly possible.

Until my brother managed to usher her outside, to a more appropriate place to cry – guided to the bottom of the stairwell and outside the boat club (I don't boat, sail or do anything remotely yachty; it was just a decent place to have a party).

Eventually, she relented, gathered her thoughts and strutted back toward the party. Cake in hand, gaunt from spending the best part of an hour publicly weeping, she recommenced her cakely duties. "Would you like some apple cake? I made it myself."

Her apple cake was amazing. Not worth the public embarrassment of having my mother cry the entire way through my engagement party, but not far off it.

Myself and my fiancée split up a year or so later, after a fairly dramatic ending and tumultuous few years. Turns out my mum was right to disapprove… although she could have chosen a less theatrical way of going about it. I almost respect her candour!

"A mother always knows" was one of her favourite go-to parables. I'm not sure if that line was supposed to come across as a life lesson or a threat; with her, most things carried some element of threat/spite/vehement disdain, so I reckon it wasn't a life lesson kind of statement.

Until my wedding to Rezanne in 2018, when in her impromptu speech she ended with the same line: "I know because I'm his mother." A variation on a theme of threat, I like to think this was more in the vein of approval, rather than the usual dose of spite, because she loved my wife. My mum's speech was more of a roast than my best man's, switching between embarrassing story, maternal lecture and general forthrightness. She did a good job.

We moved our wedding forward for her. The pancreatic cancer had spread, and the doctors had told us, if we wanted her to see the wedding, we'd better get it done in the next three months, if not less. We organized the entire wedding in seven weeks, without underlying hostility.

She smiled, she cried, she socialized. Maybe she actually liked me? Or just liked my wife, Rezanne… Yeah, it's probably that.

Chapter 18

The Beating on the Beach

After my mum's funeral and quasi-wake, myself, my dad, Nate and Rezanne made our way back to our family home, closely followed by my Aunt Lis and Uncle Nigel.

By this point, there was an air of relief that the hardest part of the day was over. We made our way to the garden and perched on broken chairs laid out on unmown grass, drinking tea from brown-stained teacups.

My chair tilted to the back-left, forcing me to lean upward whilst balancing on my left leg. I wasn't really sitting, more attempting not to fall onto the giant cat litter Poppy had inhabited and marked as her own. The garden of 42 Ripstone Gardens was covered in cat poo and dead mice, in equal measure. She sat proudly upright in front of her toilet-cumhunting-ground: "Yeah, I did that… and that!! Yes, and that!" We would bury her in the same garden six months later, next to Pushkin. Nate would carry her body in a shoe box, from London to Southampton, that December.

Laid to rest amongst her prey and other dead pets.

Later in the afternoon, myself, Rezanne and Lis made our way to the front room, to sort through my mum's homemade jewellery. "The Earring Lady" was my mum's alter-ego. Moonlighting as an artisan, she sold her jewellery at fayres and fêtes. Boxes full of necklaces and earrings remain unsold in my brother's store cupboards. Eventually, we will sort through them all and make some attempt at selling them, or simply donating them.

Before the funeral, Rezanne had the idea of giving a piece of mum's jewellery to all of the women who were invited to the funeral. Each was asked for their preference in terms of stone and colour, and a box presented to each at the reception.

Lis always wore flamboyant colours, from head to toe, decked out in bright-purple, velvet hats and equally bright, orange-and-turquoise scarves (and occasionally more than one scarf, depending on the occasion). So, we were slightly perplexed when her memento request was for a necklace in full dark stone: haematite. I asked her if she was sure, and she replied that she was very much into that kind of thing nowadays. Sure enough, there it was, buried at the bottom of a bag of jewellery boxes: a full haematite necklace. We packed and labelled it *"Auntie Lis"*.

At the reception, each of the women opened their mementoes and Lis followed suit.

"Oh, no, I don't like this," she bellowed out, for all to hear!

One of the other ladies present tried to hush her protestations: "Lis, you can't say that!" She always spoke her mind, regardless of the occasion, hence the graveside critique of my love life.

"Lis, this is exactly what you asked for," I replied.

"Ohhhh, no, I just remembered, it was a friend of mine who likes haematite, not me."

Puzzled by this response of not knowing whether she or her friend liked something, I simply laughed it off and returned to mingling amongst the guests scattered across the socially distanced gazebo, in a family friend's garden (our garden definitely wasn't fit to host humans; only cats and immediate family could brave that terrain).

After having propped myself upright for the best part of an hour, myself, Rezanne and my aunt made our way to the front room, to sort through the bags and boxes of The Earring Lady's legacy. Turquoise bracelets, haematite pendants, faux pearl earrings... box after box, bag after bag... My aunt picked out her favourites to take home with her, filing them to one side; I pictured my mum turning in her very new grave, sickened by the thought of her nemesis pillaging through her property.

I took little notice and left her to loot in peace. I sat in the corner of the room, sorting through old magazines and piles of unidentified belongings, while Rezanne pawed through another bag of jewellery, attempting to find what could be worn by her or her sister/mother/aunt/other female friend and/or relative.

Through the rustling and occasional dust-induced sneezes, I detected the faint sound of sobbing coming from my aunt's direction. It became louder!

I looked over. "Lis, what's wrong?"

"I can't ever forgive myself."

"Forgive yourself for what, Lis?"

"It was on Bournemouth beach, when you were just a little boy."

"What was?"

Rezanne looked just as confused as I did. Or maybe she was confused that I looked confused.

"She— she—" (inaudible sound followed by sobs, followed by more sounds) "she beat you."

"I'm sorry, what?"

"She beat you and I did nothing!"

"Lis, I don't know what you're talking about."

"On the beach. You don't remember?! I stood by and did nothing… and you were just a boy. I mean, we had different parenting styles – that's a certainty – but you were just a boy."

"I honestly don't remember, Lis. I'm sorry." For some reason, I apologized for not remembering. It felt like the right thing to do in the circumstances.

I comforted my aunt, cuddling her back as she bawled her eyes out about my dead mother beating me, thirty years ago, on a beach. And me not remembering any of it.

Did it happen? Did I block it out?

Regardless, I looked over at Rezanne, trying not to laugh about how ridiculous it was that, having just buried my mother, I would have to stand there comforting others, as they recanted tales of my public flogging at the seaside.

Eventually, the sobbing subsided, and we could continue with the sorting and sifting of what remained of The Earring Lady's work.

The beating on the beach lives on in infamy, as the greatest beating I never had.

Although, my brother and I would often get the slipper: a smelly, white Scholl, with one off-white strap and a buckle. And a slightly raised, rubberized heel, for extra welly.

I can picture the slipper as if it were yesterday.

Always threatened with a slippering, we were subdued into cooperation through fear. If we misbehaved – which was a broad term with my mum, and could mean talking, breathing, eating or just existing – it would no doubt result in a slippering on the backside once we got home.

It got to the stage where we quite liked it. Some weird, juvenile Stockholm Syndrome perpetuated throughout 42 Ripstone Gardens.

"Right, that's it. If you misbehave again I'll get the slipper… I will!"

Nonchalantly Nate and I would compete to see who could be slippered hardest.

"That doesn't even hurt, Mum. I don't care."

"Yeah," echoed Nate, "hit me again."

Tirelessly, my mum would wield the slipper of punishment. How dare her offspring show such indignation.

Bums red-raw, we battled on through gritted teeth. Eventually, Mum would relent; we'd had enough of the slipper for one day.

Funnily enough, I don't recall the slipper ever being taken to the seaside. If the beating on the beach did in fact take place, then it did not involve the slipper. Maybe a shoe?

Maybe a jelly shoe? We were forced to wear jelly shoes until our early teens, to avoid the stings of weaver fish and the like. Pasted head-to-toe in thick factor-50, we blindly ambled across the beach, struggling to the sea through sweat and sunscreen, big, white bucket hats shoved on our heads. Two scrawny,

Speedo-clad Jewish boys bouncing about Bournemouth beach after a summer Cheder class (Jewish Sunday School), or after seeing my grandparents in the old retirement flats, on the cliffs above the sea front.

Chapter 19
The Orphan

Can you be orphaned at thirty-five? Is there a cut-off date, or is the phrase solely reserved for children?

According to *Collins Dictionary Online*:

"Word forms – plural, 3rd person, singular, present tense: orphans; past tense: orphaned

1. COUNTABLE NOUN

An orphan is a child whose parents are dead.

'I'm an orphan and pretty much grew up on my own.'

'...a young orphan girl brought up by peasants.'

2. PASSIVE VERB [no cont.]

If a child is orphaned, their parents die or their remaining parent dies."[2]

So, that settles it: I lost the right to call myself an orphan upon turning eighteen. So, what are we adults who lose our parents

---

[2] *https://www.collinsdictionary.com/dictionary/english/orphan*

called? Are we just adults? Is losing a parent/parents simply part of adulthood?

It feels like we're expected to just get on with it. Take your compassionate leave and put on a brave face, whilst secretly masking all that inner torment and pain, and all the other shit.

Grief is unique to everyone, but one thing it will always be is lingering. It hangs at the back of your mind, haunts and torments. Maybe you can come to terms with it and accept whatever the loss left you with, but it will always be there. I don't ever see mine going, and to be honest I don't want it to; if it's gone then they're gone, and I don't want that.

My grief is unresolved for my own reasons. I missed both of my parents dying.

I've phrased that in a way that sounds like I have some kind of morbid FOMO, but I did miss it; I wasn't there. I held my dad's hand for ten hours and then I left; thirty minutes later I was called by the hospital to say that he had passed. I was in the hallway of my and Rezanne's flat when my phone rang. I instantly knew it was the hospital.

"I'm sorry to say that your father passed around five minutes ago."

Why didn't I stay half an hour longer? I didn't need to leave. I was just tired; I could have stayed. I could have been there for him to help him. He wasn't conscious, but he knew I was there – I could feel it. I felt his awareness of me.

My back to the hallway wall, my legs crumpled beneath me as the news took hold, and tears ran down my face.

The doctor said to us that sometimes they hang on until everyone has left, and then they go – "they" being "the-aboutto-die". "The-about-to-die" will hang on, even if there's nothing to hang on for. The desire to live survives within your subconscious, even if the conscious mind has long left the body. He hung on.

I held his hand. It was hot. It made him seem full of life. How could someone so warm have no life left in them? His eyes flickered as my wife stroked his hair. I wanted him to die with me there; I didn't want him to die alone. That saying, "we all die alone," isn't true; you can be surrounded by the people you love and who love you. But he died alone because of me. Those are my demons, my unresolved grief issues. I let my dad die alone because I was tired.

We found a stray radio in the Covid ward and propped it up on the windowsill, tuned into Classic FM, and left him with his favourite music, as he drifted off out to sea. It was calm. The current did cease. He closed his eyes, breathed in… For now, he was at peace.

Chapter 20
Full Circle

So, the bagel and the boiled egg...

Life is round, according to the rabbi, just like the egg and just like the bagel. But I wanted to know a little more about this tradition, although it seemed fairly self-explanatory. As such, I went onto *Chabad Online*, for some sagely Yiddisher wisdom on this ancient ritual.

Just in case you ever wondered about the halachic (Jewish law) reasoning behind this particular Judaic funereal tradition:

"The first meal that the mourners eat after the funeral is called the Seudat Havra'ah [3] *(literally "Meal of Recovery"). According to Jewish law, they generally do not eat their own food, but instead eat a meal provided by neighbors, relatives or the community."*

---

[3] The name stems from the verse in II Samuel 3:35, which describes how the people brought a meal to King David when he was mourning the death of Abner.

This concept is found in Scripture, where we read how God told the prophet Ezekiel about the impending destruction of the Holy Temple. To drive home the point, He also told the

---

prophet that his wife would pass away, but *"a mourning for the dead you shall not make... and put your shoes on your feet... and you shall not eat the bread of men."*[4]

From here, the Talmud [4] understands that under ordinary circumstances the mourners would eat food provided by others *("the bread of man")*. The primary foods eaten at this meal are bagels (or round rolls), (peeled) [5] hard-boiled eggs and/or lentils.[6]

JACOB COOKS LENTILS

The custom of giving round foods is learned from Jacob, who cooked a pot of lentils. The sages say that this was to console his father Isaac, after the death of his own father, Abraham.[7] The Talmud[8] offers two reasons for this custom.

---

[4] Talmud, Moed Katan 27b.

[5] See Beit Yosef, Yoreh De'ah 378 in Bedek Habayit, quoting the Orchot Chaim, and Rabbi Akiva Eiger on 378. The reason it is peeled is so that the mourners do not appear ravenous when they peel it themselves.

[6] Talmud, Bava Batra 16b; Shulchan Aruch, Orach Chaim 552:8; Yoreh De'ah 378:1.

[7] See Genesis 25:29-20 and Rashi ad loc.

[8] Talmud, Bava Batra 16b.

Just as this lentil has no mouth (i.e., it does not have a crack, like other legumes), so too a mourner has no mouth (that is, his anguish prevents him from speaking).

Alternatively, just as this lentil is completely round, so too mourning comes around to the inhabitants of the world (e.g., it is part of the cycle of life, and eventually reaches all).

The Talmud explains that the difference between the two explanations is whether one can use an egg, since it is not completely round. Practically, the custom is to use an egg (and some also serve lentils).

THE RESURRECTION

Another reason for using the egg is that, while it may appear to be a completed object, it is just a preparation for the live creature that emerges from it.

This symbolizes our faith and hope for the future. For, although our loved one just passed away, we believe, hope and pray for the fulfilment of the verse, *"He will swallow up death forever; and the Lord God will wipe away tears from off all faces... For death is not final. When the Moshiach comes, the dead will be resurrected, and we will once again be reunited with our loved ones.*

"May it be speedily in our days!"[10] [9]

I'm going to read into the egg thing in a slightly less messianic interpretation (sorry, Maimonides, or whichever other Talmuddic scholar is responsible for the above). Life, death, birth, burial and the rituals constantly cycle in life's perpetual motion. We all stumble, amble, struggle, hurt, cry, strive and end. And then it starts all over again – not some messianic rebirth of the dead, like some Jewish zombie apocalypse.

Spielberg's Yiddish version of *Train to Busan* isn't something I want to experience any time soon. The dead should stay dead; messianic intervention is not required anywhere, ever.

No, the egg is surely representative of birth. That, although life comes to an end, life will follow. It is not an end, and although our own existence is finite, it continues in others. My dad's existence continues within me; my mum's existence continues within me. We don't die entirely; we leave something behind. My mum might have been a little more hard-boiled than the average egg, and my dad a little more scrambled, and after all

---

[9] *https://www.chabad.org/library/article_cdo/aid/5280422/jewish/Why-Are-Mourners-Served-Bagels-and-Eggs.htm*
10 *Minhagei Yeshurun, 212.*

of this I'm a little fried… but, all that we leave behind – all that love, all that life – means something, albeit intangible.

So, Mum and Dad, in the spirit of all that we leave behind, meet your grandchild, the newest Davis egg…

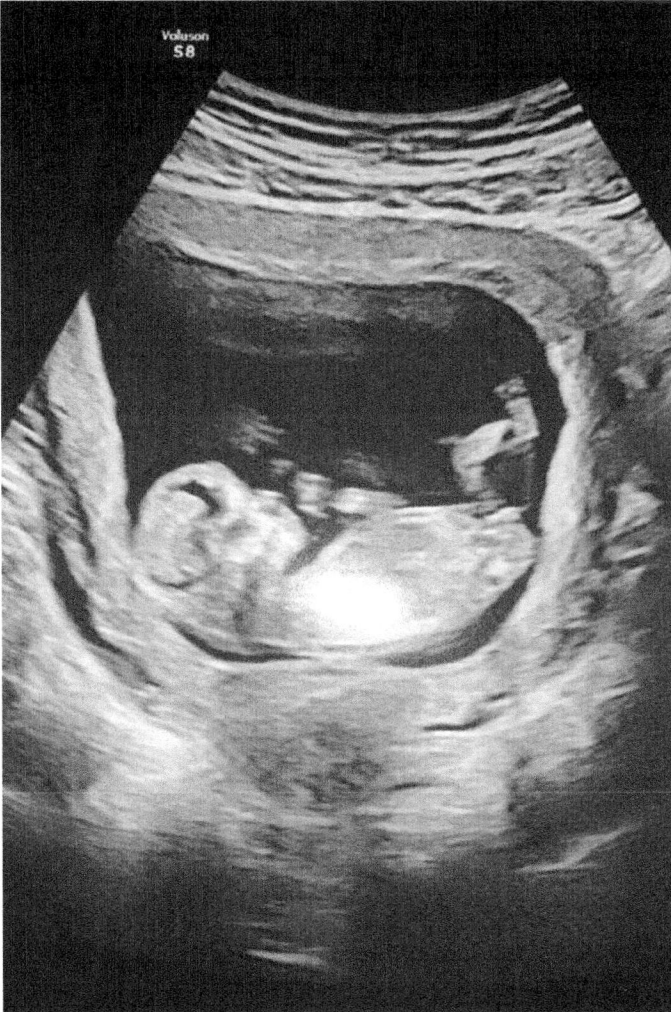

THE END.

ACKNOWLEDGEMENTS

I would like to thank all those who helped me along this journey. Rania Mattar and Daniel Dalton for being my early stage editors, when I didn't even know if what I had written made an kind of cohesive sense. To my wife, Rezanne Mattar, who has been there through all the ups and downs one can possibly experience when dealing with the loss of parents, long lost siblings and family pets.

Most of all – I would like to posthumously thank my dad. It was his passion for literature; more specifically poetry that started me on this journey. Always head-down, buried in whatever book had sparked his interest in the local charity book section of Help the Aged or Oxfam. Books were always turning up, strewn over the living room floor, or shoved in a coat pocket. Without this constant inadvertent exposure I wouldn't have started this project. Reading and writing became part of my earlier life because of him – and perhaps losing him drove me to finish a book that I might not have had the drive to complete but for this heavy loss.

To his poet's soul – the rest is silent.

ABOUT THE AUTHOR

J S Davis was born in Southampton in 1985. Having spent the entirety of his early life in the Southampton area, he attended the Gregg School before studying his A levels at Peter Symonds College in Winchester. It was during these school years that he developed his love for drama and literature.

After several failed attempts to follow his heart by pursuing his passions for art and sport by briefly attending Art School at Southampton University; then moving onto several offers of American University soccer scholarships, he opted for a more pragmatic direction - leaving the South Coast to study Law at Nottingham Trent University.

Having graduated, he spent two and a half years teaching English as a foreign language in Thailand, Cambodia and Italy, before returning to complete a Post Graduate Diploma in Legal Practice at Cardiff University. Upon graduation he found employment in law firms in Cardiff and qualified as a solicitor. He subsequently moved to London where he practiced criminal defence and completed a master's degree in Legal Practice. He currently practices criminal law in South Wales.

He married his wife Rezanne in 2018, and their first child, Rosa was born in the summer of 2022.

This is J S Davis' first published book – his tribute to his parents.

Printed in Great Britain
by Amazon

62436651R00068